Ad Break

Written by Susan Griffiths
Illustrated by Kelvin Hucker

| Contents | Page |

Chapter 1.   4
I hate ads

Chapter 2.   6
Research

Chapter 3.   10
The disgusting drink

Chapter 4.   18
Poor Uncle Seymour

Chapter 5.   24
The great discovery

Chapter 6.   28
Success!

Verse   32

Rigby

Ad Break

With these characters ...

Kristina

Mom

Damien

Uncle Seymour

Setting the scene ...

If you're tired of watching so many ads on TV, spare a thought for poor Kristina. Her Uncle Seymour is one of the people who make those ads, and he asks her to try out the dumbest things! As if that's not bad enough, she also has to put up with a very dumb brother who has very stinky sneakers! Just when Kristina thought that life couldn't get much worse, Uncle Seymour turns up again to prove her wrong.

breathtaking!"

Chapter 1.

If you are like me, you hate advertisements on TV! Interrupting your favorite program, trying to sell you stuff you don't want. Have you ever wondered who makes those advertisements? Well, I know someone. My Uncle Seymour. He made advertisements for TV. I say "made" because he doesn't do that anymore. He became very rich and now lives near the beach in Hawaii—all because of something I discovered. But I will tell you the whole story, just the way it happened.

Chapter 2.

My name is Kristina, and I could spend ages telling you about the dumb things I've had to try out for Uncle Seymour. You see, he tried out all the new things on me before he made the advertisements. He called it "research." I called it "cruelty."

My older brother, Damien, never got roped in for "research." I guess Uncle Seymour thought my brother was too hopeless to ask *him* anything sensible! My brother really is wacky!

Every time I heard Uncle Seymour drive up to our house and run excitedly up the driveway, I knew that I was about to be "researched."

"Kristina!" called my mom. "Uncle Seymour has some questions to ask you."

Here are just some of the things I've had to research: I've had to taste an indescribable purple-colored milk drink, eat indigestible chocolate-flavored bologna, and chew some inedible cauliflower-flavored jelly beans. Each time, I had to secretly spit it out! Grown-ups don't know the first thing about what we kids want!

"Kristina."

Purple-colored milk, chocolate-flavored bologna, and cauliflower-flavored jelly beans, I do *not* need! Give me a glass of milk, normal bologna, and a bag of ordinary jelly beans anytime, I say.

Anyway, the last time Uncle Seymour visited our house, I got the dreaded call.

Chapter 3.

"How come Damien never has to do this?" I muttered, as I moped down the hallway. "It's not fair!"

"Hi, Kristina!" greeted Uncle Seymour. "Have *I* got something for *you!*"

"I thought you might," I muttered again, rolling my eyes.

It was a powdered, fruit-flavored drink. I was going to ask Uncle Seymour why anyone would want that when they could buy great fresh juice, but I didn't want to hurt his feelings.

"I'm getting a lot of money from the Powerful Powder company to make some advertisements that will make everyone want to buy this drink," he said. "So, I need to know what you think of it."

Mom mixed up the drink and brought me a glass. It looked like the aspirin drink that Mom makes whenever she gets a throbbing headache. (That's usually right after Damien plays his CDs too loud.)

I looked suspiciously at the drink. At least it wasn't purple! I sniffed it and looked at Uncle Seymour. He was watching me very closely. It smelled like my brother's stinky sneakers. "Well," I said, "here goes . . ."

I took a sip and just about fell over. It was like sucking a lemon! It was so strong that I screwed up my face and gasped for air. It was sour and bitter and horrible!

"It's great, huh?" grinned Uncle Seymour. "You like it?"

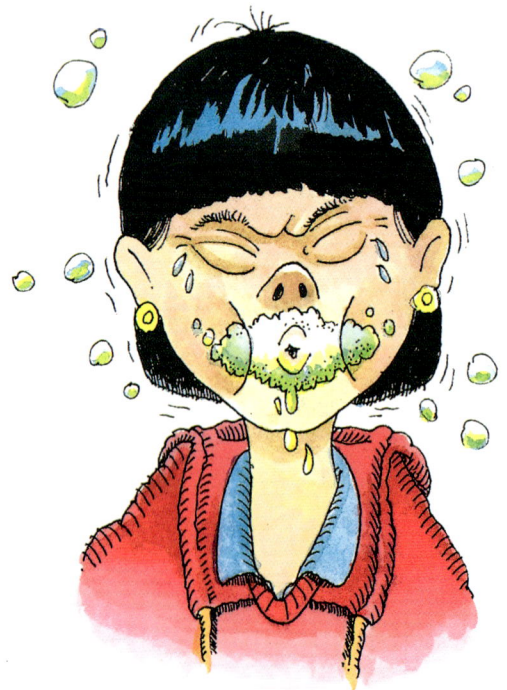

I tried hard to think of something nice to say.

"It's . . . it's . . . it's breathtaking!" I whispered. At least *that* was true.

Uncle Seymour stood up and clapped his hands.

"That's a great slogan," he said. "That's what we'll use in our advertising! We'll say, 'It's Breathtaking!'"

Uncle Seymour left us with a dozen packages of the powdered drink and rushed out to his car.

"It's breathtaking," he kept saying. "Breathtaking!"

While Mom wasn't looking, I took the packages and hid them in the bathroom. I didn't want her mixing up any more of that stuff, thank you very much. I'd had enough of my breath taken for one day!

Chapter 4.

Soon enough, we saw the advertisements on TV. A famous actor was drinking a huge glass of the drink, smiling, and saying, "It's Breathtaking!" I bet they didn't have a video of him spitting it out afterward and making a face!

The trouble was, no one liked the drink. I certainly wasn't surprised. Uncle Seymour called on the telephone a couple of weeks later, sounding very worried.

"No one likes our drink," he moaned. "I won't get any money. The people at the Powerful Powder company are saying that no one wants to buy the drink because I made a bad ad. What am I going to do?"

Just then, Damien walked in. I knew he was coming because I could smell his stinky sneakers from down in the hallway.

"Pooh, Damien!" I said. "What have you been walking in?"

Mom screwed up her nose, too.

"Go and put some lemon and lavender talcum powder in your sneakers," she said. Damien disappeared into the bathroom.

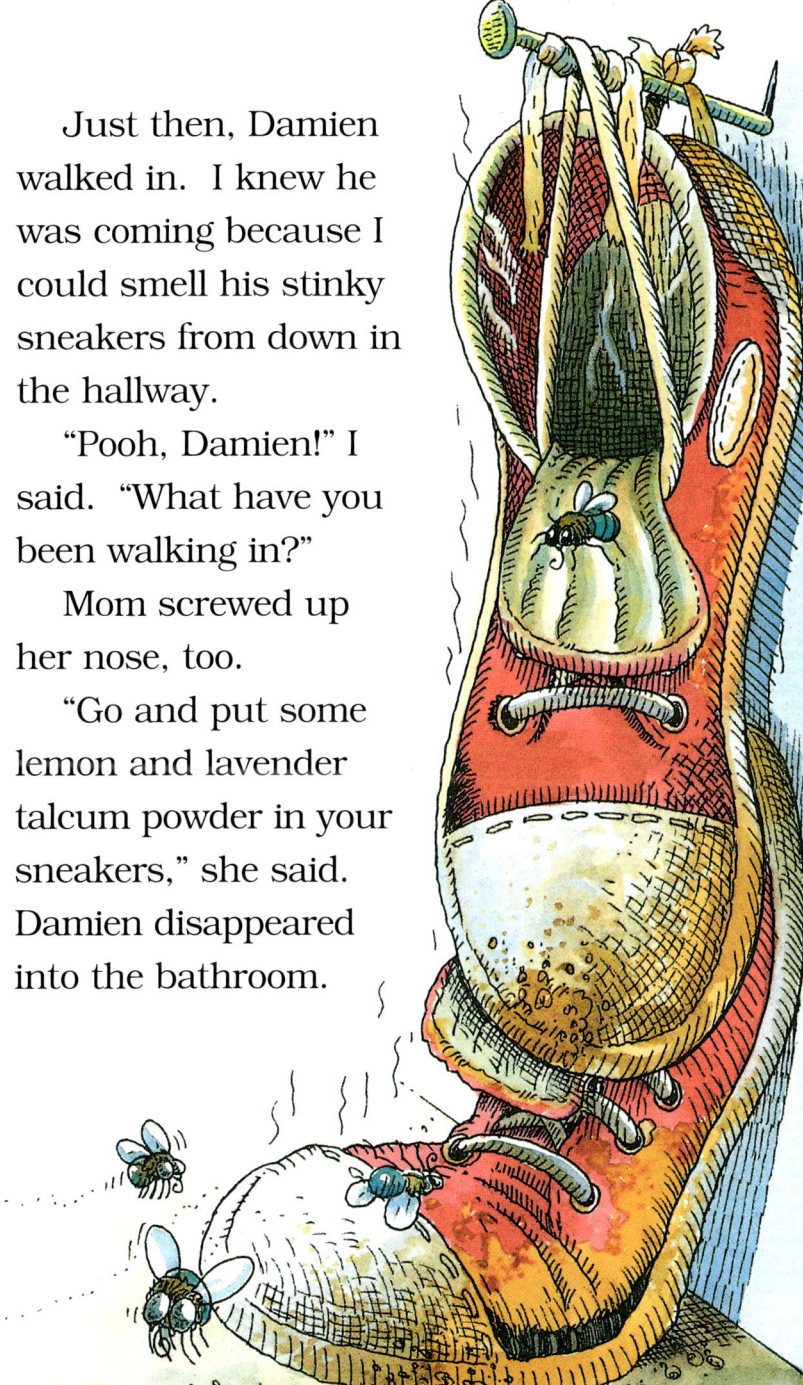

Mom finished talking to Uncle Seymour, and I sat there wondering what would be next on Uncle Seymour's list of great ideas.

We didn't hear anything from Uncle Seymour for a week.

I don't think anyone wanted him to make any more advertisements, because the last one had been so disastrous. I was secretly quite glad.

Then I made my great discovery!

Chapter 5.

We were all sitting down to dinner one night—Damien, Mom, and I. Something wasn't quite right, but it took me a while to think of what it was. I sniffed. I sniffed again.

"Can you smell anything?" I said.

Mom looked up. "Smell?" she asked. "I can't smell anything."

"Neither can I," I said. *That* was what was so unusual.

We both looked at Damien. Then we both looked at Damien's feet. Sure enough, he had his stinky old sneakers on. But there wasn't even the slightest whiff coming from them.

"I've been using that new talcum powder in the bathroom," he said proudly. "The stuff that Uncle Seymour left. It's good, isn't it!"

"That's not talcum powder," I laughed. "That's . . . ," I stopped. I had my great idea.

I called Uncle Seymour.

"Hey, Uncle Seymour," I said. "What would you do if you were really, *really* rich?"

"I'd go and live on a beach in Hawaii for a long, long time," he replied.

"Really?" I said. "You wouldn't make any more ads?"

"Nope," he said.

"You wouldn't need to test any more stuff on me?" I asked.

"No way," he said. "I wouldn't do *anything!*"

So I told him my idea.

Chapter 6.

Soon enough, we saw the ads on TV. A famous actor was sprinkling a package of the drink powder into his sneakers. He smiled and sniffed the sneakers. Then a famous actress came on, sniffed his sneakers, and gave him a huge, sloppy kiss.

"Yuck!" I thought.

People went crazy. Everyone had to buy the new sneaker-smell remover. The people at the Powerful Powder company became fabulously rich. And my dear old Uncle Seymour became rich, too.

Sure enough, just like he promised, he bought himself a ticket to Hawaii, and I've been safe from purple milk drinks, chocolate-flavored bologna, and powdered drinks ever since. All it took was a little bit of *real* research! That, and my brother's *breathtakingly b-a-d* sneakers.

"It's breathtaking!"

Poor Uncle Seymour was very sad,
No one seemed to like his brand new ad.

But then I had a most brilliant idea,
That brought Uncle Seymour happiness and cheer.

"The product," I said, "much better than a drink,
Achieves great results in reducing a stink!"